Original title:
Life's Meaning: Shrouded in Mystery

Copyright © 2025 Creative Arts Management OÜ
All rights reserved.

Author: Lila Davenport
ISBN HARDBACK: 978-1-80566-162-7
ISBN PAPERBACK: 978-1-80566-457-4

Sifting Through the Sands of Perception

In a world of socks that do not match,
We ponder truths we can't quite catch.
Like cats with laser dots to chase,
We stumble through this endless space.

Chasing fortune in a cereal bowl,
With every spoon, we lose control.
The milk and marshmallows swirl about,
While we in wonder, laugh and shout.

A rubber chicken sings a tune,
Underneath the pale, bright moon.
We treat our doubts like a magic trick,
Making sense can be quite slick.

So let's toast to questions left unsaid,
And dance on dreams we once had fled.
With every giggle, we may find,
The joy in chaos, never blind.

The Puzzle of Being

Why's a ladder always near?
To reach the thoughts we fear.
Missing pieces in our game,
Socks and chairs, all look the same.

Is the cat a mystic sage?
Wiping down the coffee page?
Every mirror tells a joke,
Wish it would, but it just spoke.

Wandering Through Questions

Why does cheese and wisdom pair?
Is there magic in the air?
Chasing shadows, chasing light,
Oh, this riddle's quite a sight!

Do fish think about their fins?
Or do they dream of lost chins?
I asked a tree, it said, "Beleaf!"
Then it chuckled like a thief.

A Symphony of Doubts

The toaster plays a serenade,
While socks are having a parade.
Bananas whisper strange tunes,
As the tablecloth swoons.

Questions dance like worn-out shoes,
On the floor, they sound like blues.
Tick-tock clocks, they laugh and tease,
While my mind's a jigsaw, please!

The Art of Unraveling

What's the point of a round pizza?
Is it hiding from a feature?
Spaghetti dreams of winding roads,
While the fork pretends it knows.

Do we wear hats just for fun?
Or to hide from the sun?
In the chaos, we all sway,
Juggling puzzles every day.

Secrets of the Infinite

Why do socks always vanish?
They join some secret club, you see.
Their mission? To stay hidden and sly,
While we search with all our glee.

If truth were a jigsaw, edge pieces first,
Finding corners would drive us all mad.
We'd end up with a puzzling picture,
Of a cat wearing a tutu, quite bad.

What's the purpose of a spilled drink?
A chance for jokes in every spill.
Perhaps it's a secret world of whimsy,
Where puddles teach us to chill.

In dreams we chase elusive truths,
With spaghetti monsters, oh so neat.
They laugh as we tumble, curious fools,
Just trying to find our own two feet.

The Puzzle of Existence

Once I met a wise old tree,
He whispered secrets of the breeze.
I asked him why he was so tall,
He chuckled, 'Photosynthesis, please!'

Life's a puzzle, missing pieces,
Like my lunch, gone without a trace.
Maybe it's hiding in a drawer,
With my missing socks in some wild race.

I asked a cat about the stars,
He blinked and licked his paws with pride.
'You think they're bright? I think they're snacks,
Floating there, no need to hide!'

If questions were flavors, mine would be sweet,
With chocolate sauce on every bite.
But answers often taste like spinach,
At least the jokes are out of sight!

Fragments of Untold Stories

In a world where ants wear hats,
Who knows what secrets they might share?
Perhaps they're plotting a grand surprise,
To banish all the humans' despair.

I found a bird with a broken wing,
He said, 'Life's not all bad, my mate!'
With every chirp, a tale unfolds,
About the worms he plans to bait.

What's hiding in the cookie jar?
A history of crumbs and sins.
Each nibble takes us back in time,
To when the baker first began his wins.

Mystery wraps us like a blanket,
In each wrinkle, laughs wait in store.
So let's embrace this tangled riddle,
As we dance through the open door.

Wading Through the Fog

Fog rolls in like a cotton candy dream,
Obscuring the path beneath our feet.
We stumble with purpose, arms outstretched,
Like blindfolded geese in sync, so sweet.

What's hiding in the depths of haze?
Maybe a party of ghostly fun.
They toast to questions, dance with glee,
While we wonder if we've ever won.

With every step, a funny slip,
We laugh as we fumble and sway.
Existence is just a grand old joke,
Best told in a fog of disarray.

So let's twirl in this mysterious dance,
With giggles echoing through the air.
As fog thickens, we'll play our part,
Wading through unknowns without a care.

Chasing Phantoms

In the dance of shadows we prance,
With capes and hats, we take a chance.
Ghosts in the attic, they tease and they poke,
Yet here we are, lost in a joke.

Searching for meaning in a spilled cup,
Drowning our woes, we lift it up.
Tables all wobble, laughter is loud,
Around every corner, a question avowed.

Beneath the Clandestine Sky

Beneath the sky with secrets to keep,
Aliens giggle while others just sleep.
Stars twinkle like winks, conspiracies start,
But I'm lost just trying to pick apart.

What does it mean when ducks all row?
They quack in code, but I don't know.
Mystery socks in a laundry race,
Are they sentient? Could it be so? What a chase!

Threads of the Unconscious

Pulling at threads of a puzzling scheme,
Wake up, they whispered, it's all just a dream.
Floating through colors all tangled and bright,
Is that a shadow? Or just a light bite?

Caught in the web of a spider's delight,
Falling for truths hidden out of sight.
What's really out there? I'd like to know,
But the mirror just laughs at my bravado.

A Tapestry of Illusions

A tapestry woven with yarns of the weird,
What's real or not? Honestly, I've feared.
Unraveled by thoughts that tickle my brain,
It's all a joke, like a runaway train.

Weaving through nonsense, shimmery and bright,
I'll take a detour, avoiding the fright.
Pulling the strings with a mischievous cheer,
In this grand circus, everyone's dear.

The Veil Between Moments

In a world where time can stall,
We trip on pants, we miss the call.
A sneeze might start a great debate,
Is that cloud a sign of fate?

Our socks don't match, yet we still stride,
Chasing crumbs where secrets hide.
With laughter loud, we make our way,
Why find answers? Let's just play!

Echoes of the Unknown

The fridge hums like a mystery,
Should I eat that? It's history!
An odd noise from the car I drive,
Could it be that gremlins thrive?

My cat stares deep, a gaze so sly,
Is he a sage, or just a guy?
In jokes, we find our fabled keys,
Unlocking doors, yet losing keys!

Quest for Clarity

A map in hand, we plot our route,
But paths get tangled. What a hoot!
With every turn, a laugh or two,
Lost in thoughts that feel so new.

Google tells me I'm not alone,
Yet my GPS just moans and groans.
In puzzling quests, there's fun to gain,
Frustration blooms, a silly strain.

Beneath the Surface Stillness

Beneath the calm, the fish may dance,
In swirling waves, they take a chance.
Do they know secrets we can't see?
Or just swim around with glee?

The quiet ponds may speak in dreams,
While frogs in tuxes plot their schemes.
Nature's whispers, at times absurd,
Are they wise, or just plain weird?

Pulse of the Infinite

In the heart of a cat's yawn,
We ponder the stars' view.
Is it wisdom or just a prank,
Inviting us to ask, who knew?

A banana slipped on the floor,
Fates twist and turn with glee.
Is that an omen from above,
Or just my clumsiness, oh me!

Mists of Intuition

Cabbage in a crisp salad,
Feels profound in my thoughts.
Is it the dressing or fortune?
Both could be true, says the dots.

The dog stares, deep in my soul,
With a wag and a tilt of head.
Says he knows why we're all here,
But his tennis ball's still unled!

The Dappled Light of Insight

A lamp flickers; shadows dance,
Are we actors stuck on pause?
Or simply lost in the glow,
Chasing sparks without a cause?

The toaster and I share secrets,
Golden bread is our muse.
Is it crunch that makes us giggle,
Or deep thoughts we can't choose?

Unfurling the Riddles

The clock ticks, yet won't reveal,
Why socks vanish from the wash.
Is it time playing hide-and-seek?
Or just my dry cleaning mishmash?

The fish swims, eyes full of dreams,
In its bowl, seeks to confide.
But all I hear is bubbling bliss,
As it plans a fishy glide!

The Question in Every Heart

Why do socks disappear like smoke,
Leaving us with pairs that can't invoke?
Is it a plot from laundry elves?
Or just our minds playing with shelves?

We ponder truth in fruitless debates,
While munching on cookies that silence fates.
Do fish know why they swim in schools?
Or is it all just a game of fools?

Horizons Yet to Be Trod

Underneath the stars, we make our plans,
With glittering dreams held in tiny hands.
Is the sky blue or just our minds?
Or do we see what the universe finds?

We tiptoe on paths that twist and turn,
Searching for bridges that rarely burn.
Do the chickens cross roads to find their quest?
Or just to cluck at the clothes we dress?

Dancing with Ambivalence

In a room full of shadows, we waltz with flair,
Applauding the silence that fills up the air.
Do we chase after dreams or let them stay?
As squirrels in the park just steal our spray.

With snacks in hand, we spin to the tune,
Trying to figure out the craters on the moon.
Is it cheese or a ruse from aliens above?
Or simply a pizza, holding a grudge?

Reflections on the Edge

Peering down the well, we see a face,
Wondering which one chose this place.
Is it me, or am I just a figment?
A brain playing tricks as a fun segment?

The mirror laughs back with a wink and a grin,
Cashier of secrets that spin from within.
In this playful jest, what's truth, what's game?
Maybe it's all just a whimsical flame.

The Color of Abstruse Truths

Why's the sky blue, I often ponder,
Is it the ocean's great wonder?
Is a banana really a fruit?
Or just a yellow, bendy brute?

Does grass grow under a tree's shade?
Or does it play a sneaky charade?
Questions floating like clouds on a spree,
Tickling my mind, oh, the irony!

Uncharted Waters of Thought

Sailing seas of thoughts so wide,
With a rubber ducky as my guide.
Do fish speak in gurgles and swirls?
Or prefer the company of pearls?

In this boat, my mind can drift,
Navigating with a magical lift.
Finding answers in jellybean dreams,
And realizing nothing's what it seems!

In the Company of Questions

What if cats ruled the world today?
Would they meow in a charming way?
Do trees gossip about our lives?
Whispering secrets as each one thrives?

Do socks long to find their lost pairs?
Or do they dance in forgotten lairs?
In this jigsaw of curious spins,
Each piece wears a grin, where laughter begins!

The Flickering Flame of Inquiry

From candlelight, ideas blaze bright,
Why does the fridge hum all night?
Is time a cat with nine cozy lives?
Or just a clock that occasionally dives?

With every flicker, I sense anew,
Questions swirl in a playful queue.
Finding humor in the great unknown,
In this comedy where doubts are sown!

The Boundary Where Light Meets Dark

In the twilight, shadows play,
Chasing light, they run away.
Mixing giggles with a sigh,
Wondering when and how to fly.

A rooster crows, it's just a dream,
Splashing colors in the stream.
Chickens pondering where to go,
And pigs in tuxedos steal the show.

Mice hold court with tiny hats,
Discussions on the pros of bats.
The sun rolls its sleepy eyes,
As night unveils its grand surprise.

Finding sense in all the fun,
Where does one begin or run?
In between both dark and bright,
Jesters dance in the fading light.

Beneath the Surface of Still Waters

In a puddle, grand ideas swim,
Frog philosophers sing a hymn.
Questioning fate in croaky tones,
As turtles spin tales of their bones.

The ripples laugh, they twist and shout,
What's this fuss all about?
A goldfish tries its best to read,
A novel strung on seaweed's creed.

Reflections hide beneath the veil,
As hippos spin in a grand ballet.
Ducks are debating the state of things,
While squirrels break out tiny swing rings.

Time floats by like a gentle breeze,
With every whirl, we're sure to tease.
Beneath the calm, a chaotic dance,
Reminds us life's a funny chance.

The Uncharted Map of Wonder

Upon a map that's drawn in crayon,
X marks spots where dreams are layin'.
Llamas prance in treasure chests,
While pirates play with their own quests.

Clouds have secrets, fluffy and bright,
They whisper tales under starlit night.
Adventurers hop on bouncy springs,
As geese trade in their golden rings.

The compass spins, oh what a jest,
North is where we find the best.
With every turn, a giggle falls,
In the realm of impossible walls.

At the end of each rainbow's arc,
Hope resides with every spark.
In a world where whimsy's king,
Even the lost begin to sing.

The Allure of the Inexplicable

In a cereal box, mysteries hide,
Sugary secrets they try to bide.
Marshmallows giggle, winking an eye,
Sipping milk as they float on by.

An octopus roots for outer space,
While looking for a friendly face.
With eight arms, it juggles thoughts,
In a whirlpool of whimsical knots.

Clouds say 'hello' to wandering trees,
While flowers dance upon the breeze.
Each bloom a riddle, each petal a pratt,
Sprouting giggles where you least expect that.

Wonders waltz with a silly grin,
Chasing wishes beneath their skin.
In a world where questions entwine,
The charm of strange simply aligns.

Flickers of Awareness

In a world where ducks wear hats,
And squirrels dance waltzes with glee,
We ponder unanswerable chats,
While sipping tea with a bumblebee.

The moon plays cards with a cat,
Negotiating stars for a dance,
Mice sing operas, how about that?
In truth's great maze, we twirl and prance.

Some chase rainbows in pajamas,
While others count socks in the dark,
Are we lost in our own dramas?
Or finding joy in a dog's bark?

Yet behind the veil of everyday,
We giggle at keeping secrets,
And tickle the fate that leads astray,
In a place where laughter directs.

The Clock that Ticks Backwards

A clock on the wall says it's June,
Though it's snowing in mid-July,
Time's conundrums make us swoon,
As we catch time's tail and fly.

The sun wears sunglasses at night,
While stars in pajamas sip punch,
A perfect recipe for delight,
Every lunch is a waffle crunch!

We trip over shoes time forgot,
And waltz with shadows on the lawn,
What lessons have we all sought?
Perhaps they were never quite drawn.

As clocks spin in reverse to tease,
We find joy in the oddest places,
Like meeting a ghost with a sneeze,
And giggling at time's funny faces.

Enigmatic Journeys

Riding on bicycles made of dreams,
While jellybeans guide our way,
We unearth the riddle, it seems,
In that old penguin's cabaret.

Maps drawn in crayon lead the chase,
To treasure buried in the sand,
With squirrels as our course and grace,
And dancing lobsters, what a band!

Each twist reveals a laughing ghost,
With spaghetti streaming from its hat,
It's clear that joy's what matters most,
In this quirky, riddle-filled chat.

When fog rolls in with sugar plums,
And umbrellas become the ships,
We'll ride on rhymes where laughter hums,
And lick our lips for tasty quips!

Specters of Certainty

In a cafe where tables can talk,
And chairs gossip about the pies,
We ponder the walk of a sock,
Whose partner vanished, oh the sighs!

The raindrops recite poetry here,
While umbrellas spin tales of love,
And in this chaos, we cheer,
For cobwebs that dance with a shove.

Falling leaves giggle as they land,
Creating a quilt of bright hues,
Questioning what we understand,
As nutty squirrels play peek-a-boo.

Yet beneath this laughter and fun,
Lies a spark of wisdom and grace,
That not all answers need to be won,
In this splendid, whimsical place.

The Language of Echoing Silence

In whispers soft, the secrets play,
Like socks that vanish, day by day.
Muffled giggles in quiet halls,
What's spoken there? Just bathroom stalls.

A cat gives wisdom, with just a stare,
Its tail a scepter, no royal heir.
In silence echoes jokes unplanned,
Like scrambled eggs with jelly, how grand!

The clock ticks loud, yet time's a tease,
A dance with shadows, if you please.
We search for answers, like lost keys,
That one true word is just a sneeze.

Unveiling the Obscured

Behind the curtain, the laughter hides,
A parrot's secret, he always bides.
What's under wraps? A roguish grin,
Like the last slice of cake — we all want in!

The sun peeks shyly, then strikes a pose,
Like a rubber chicken among the pros.
Wondrous truths in pizza pie,
How many slices? Oh my, oh my!

Don't ask the sage, he's out for lunch,
Instead, we'll ponder over crunch.
With riddles baked in goofy puns,
The wisdom gained is half the fun!

Hues of Undefined Realities

A rainbow's claimed by crayons' might,
But who decided what's wrong or right?
A purple cow, quite out of place,
Is it a vehicle? Or just a face?

With shades of laughter, we'll spin around,
In dizzy circles, truths unbound.
The goldfish sways to a silent tune,
While everyone wonders if it's a boon.

A starry night with clowns and hats,
Who knew the cosmos had silly spats?
In surreal lands where oddballs roam,
What really makes a cozy home?

Secret Gardens of Understanding

In gardens lush with tangled vines,
Mystery blooms, in curious signs.
A gnome debates with clouds above,
And whispers sweetly of pizza love.

The tulips giggle, the daisies dance,
In this odd place, take a chance!
With paths that twist like curly fries,
Who said we need a map to rise?

Behind the fence, a rabbit grins,
With hidden meanings where fun begins.
In playful meadows, thoughts run wild,
Nature's humor — forever beguiled!

The Whirl of Possibility

In the whirlwind of thoughts, we spin,
Questions dance, a curious grin.
With socks mismatched, we ponder fate,
And wonder if our dreams are late.

Jellybeans fall from the sky,
Chocolate rivers, oh my, oh my!
We chase our tails, round and round,
In a circus where truths are seldom found.

Parrots squawk in debate of fate,
Declaring pancakes can truly wait.
Amidst the chaos, we find delight,
In the silly shadows of the night.

So let's toast to this baffling plot,
Where meaning hides, or maybe just forgot.
With laughter's echo, we'll never stall,
For fun's the answer, after all!

Twilight Thoughts

Beneath the stars, our minds take flight,
Wondering why cats think they're right.
A moonlit snack, with cheese and wine,
   Philosophy served on a silly line.

   Do fish ponder their fate in tanks?
   Or do they just have secret pranks?
With giggles bubbling in darkened glow,
   Twilight whispers, "You never know!"

   Lamps flicker as the crickets sing,
In this dance, what will tomorrow bring?
  The mysteries hide in shadows small,
As we trip on answers, destined to fall.

So laugh at questions that make no sense,
   As we navigate the absurd suspense.
With madness wrapped in starlit cheer,
   Each twilight thought brings us near.

Silent Ramblings

In silence, where the whispers creep,
Thoughts parade, and logic weeps.
A dog in a hat, so proud and keen,
Pondering truths that might have been.

Do clouds gossip about the sun's tan?
While squirrels plan a world-wide clan.
Our minds wander where ducks float,
On boats of wishes, they happily gloat.

The ghosts of socks lost in the wash,
Seem to conspire with the cat's sly posh.
In this comedic void of random schemes,
What's real, we ask, in our silliest dreams?

So let's celebrate this quiet spree,
With silly riddles and cups of tea.
In the mellow hush, we find the zest,
That in our thoughts, we jest the best!

The Duality of Shadows

In shadows deep where giggles hide,
A playful ghost on a broomstick ride.
It tickles the toes of logic's kin,
As we debate who gets to win.

Do shadows have stories, fair and square?
Or just trade secrets without a care?
In this paradox of light and dark,
We seek our truths, we miss the mark.

Whirlwinds of shadows, collide and clash,
While stuffed bears laugh in a delightful bash.
With ice cream dilemmas, we dine absurd,
Mixing whispers so cleverly stirred.

So raise a toast to the silly plight,
Of finding meaning in the bizarre night.
In humor's embrace, we roam so wide,
For in the dance, we take it all in stride!

The Whispering Veil

Behind the curtain, secrets play,
Mice in tuxedos dance all day.
The whispers tickle, they seem so loud,
While I just sit, lost in the crowd.

A grapefruit wearing a hat so fine,
Claims to know the world's design.
I asked it once, 'What's the grand plan?'
It just replied, 'Eat fruit, be a fan!'

The moon chuckles, it has good taste,
In hiding truths, it moves with haste.
Yet, dogs bark loudly at a passing train,
Do they know more? Or just complain?

A pickle raps on a tiny stage,
Its wisdom scribbled on the page.
All the answers are just a jest,
So bring a laugh, we need it best!

Shadows of the Unsung

In corners where the shadows loom,
A cactus sprouts in full costume.
It tells me jokes of days gone by,
While I just wonder why plants can't fly.

The lamp upon the table sighs,
Saying, 'Humans never hear the wise!'
Yet every time I check my phone,
It just scrolls memes, all alone.

A penguin lurks in a alleyway,
Sporting shades and plans for play.
He knows the secrets, a master thief,
But waddles away, just to grief.

Life's a riddle, it's all for kicks,
With fortune cookies playing tricks.
So smile wide, and let it be,
The mystery won't pay the fee.

Enigmas Beneath the Surface

Beneath the waves a fish with style,
Wears a crown, swims with a smile.
It knows the jokes of watery depth,
But I can't decode the meaning heft.

Octopus juggles thoughts so bright,
While squids recite old jokes all night.
Their tentacle wisdom bubbles up,
'Trust the salsa, not the cup!'

In the kitchen, pots have a chat,
While the fridge hums like a chubby cat.
They plot and scheme for evening meals,
Still, no one knows how hunger feels.

Turnips speak in ancient tongues,
And carrots hum their favorite songs.
So gather round, let's make a toast,
To food and laughter—the things we boast!

Threads of a Delicate Tapestry

In a loom of thoughts, the fibers twist,
An apron-wearing spider wished.
She spins her yarn of giggles sweet,
While ants join in with dancing feet.

The tapestry tells tales of wonders,
Of socks that vanish, lost in blunders.
A whisper from a shoelace says,
'Try tying me up in different ways!'

Cotton clouds float overhead,
While tangled dreams dance in my bed.
They laugh at fashion, a funny sight,
With sweaters woven a little too tight.

So here we weave our days with cheer,
As yarn and laughter intertwine, my dear.
In the grand design, we take our place,
And find our joy in a warm embrace.

Eclipsed Whispers

In shadows we dance, a curious plight,
Mysteries giggle, under moon's soft light.
Is that a cat, or my lost sock's tale?
Both are absurd, yet they never fail.

The stars are winking, they know the jest,
While coffee brews loud, I ponder the quest.
Where's the remote? It's playing a game,
Perhaps it's hiding, oh irony's fame!

Tickling curiosity, a riddle's embrace,
Finding lost keys, in a wild, frantic chase.
Life's puzzle unfolds, like a comic strip,
Each twist and turn, a slapstick quip.

Jokes abound in a world seemingly quaint,
Where wisdom wears clown shoes, oh how they paint!
So laugh at the chaos, let giggles ignite,
For in each mystery, there's pure delight!

The Enigma in Everyday

Toast pops up loud, like a jack-in-the-box,
Breakfast is strange, like wearing mismatched socks.
Why do cats stare? It's a timeless debate,
Are they plotting our doom, or just feeling great?

At the bus stop I ponder, with coffee in hand,
Why do the pigeons think they're in command?
Each honk and each squawk, a riddle's old game,
Perhaps they're just waiting for their moment of fame!

Traffic jams roar like a chaotic tin band,
While squirrels play chess, with acorns so grand.
The clock ticks like laughter, on a stubborn old wall,
With each tick and each tock, I can't help but laugh tall.

In the alley, a mural, with colors so bright,
Speaks secrets of laughter, hidden from sight.
In this puzzling dance, confusion's the muse,
Turn frowns into giggles, it's the best sort of ruse!

Secrets Beneath the Surface

Beneath the calm pond, what laughs can be found?
A duck in a tux, who swims round and round.
Water lilies gossip, in a playful disguise,
As frogs croak sonnets, beneath sapphire skies.

In kitchen cabinets, spices conspire,
Planning a banquet, entire worlds to acquire.
Salt and pepper bicker, a dash turns to fight,
Inviting the garlic, oh what sheer delight!

An empty fridge speaks tales of wild feasts missed,
While leftovers plot their revenge, coiled in mist.
Growing dusty, the wisdom lost, it seems,
What's cracked and old holds the best of our dreams.

So laugh with those secrets, with each quirky fate,
For they twist and they spin, like a jesting crate.
With riddles uncovered, let joy take its course,
In the world's funny chaos, let laughter be force!

Paradox of Existence

Why do socks vanish? A cosmic tease,
Tangled in laundry, in surreal mysteries.
The office chair creaks, whispers soft, absurd,
Is it telling jokes or just feeling disturbed?

The perplexing dance of ants marching proud,
With tiny decisions, they're never too loud.
A paper clip twists, a performer so bold,
Juggling opinions, like secrets retold.

The cat in the sunspot, lounging with flair,
Ponders existence, while flipping its hair.
Are we all just actors in a comedic play?
With laughter as punchline, to brighten our day?

In the cosmic circus, we bounce and we soar,
With puzzles galore, who could ask for more?
So grab a balloon, let the laughter ignite,
For in the unknown, we find our delight!

The Veil of Everyday Wonders

A cat that thinks she owns the chair,
While I sit on the edge, gasping for air.
My socks, they disappear one by one,
Did the dryer eat them? It's all in good fun!

A mouse that dances on the kitchen floor,
Chasing crumbs like it's got a score.
The tea kettle whistling, I'm stuck in a haze,
Is it a tune or just my crazed praise?

The neighbor's dog winks with a knowing glance,
Does he plot with the squirrels? Is it a dance?
The mailman delivers, with a grin on his face,
A world of chaos, all in its place!

My toast pops up like a jack-in-the-box,
Butterfly dreams or just silly talks?
Wonders abound in this ordinary spree,
Wrapped in a mystery, as bright as can be!

Navigating the Unseen

I tripped on my own shadow today,
Did it mean to say what it wanted to play?
The clock's tick-tock sings an offbeat tune,
Time is a jester, dressed up like a loon!

Invisible threads weave laughter in air,
Do they know I'm here, or do they just stare?
Lost and found in a world full of jest,
Navigating mysteries, what's more, what's best?

The goldfish bubbles like it's sharing a plot,
Did it just reveal secrets I've long forgot?
Or is it plotting to swim far and wide,
Join the conspiracy, take a trip with pride?

With every stumble, I learn to embrace,
A world full of humor, a quirky space.
It's clever and witty, this unseen charade,
Where laughter and joy together cascade!

Questions Wrapped in Twilight

The moon looks down, a wise old sage,
Why do socks disappear? Turn the page!
Do stars hold secrets, locked tight in their glow?
Or do they just twinkle to steal the show?

What's hiding in shadows at my front door?
The broom brigade, or a ghost from folklore?
With giggles and whispers, they set the stage,
Questions wrapped tightly in twilight's cage!

A tree with a grin, does it know what it's worth?
Does it laugh at my doubts, or rejoice at my mirth?
In every chortle, an echo of cheer,
Questions in jest, as the night draws near!

I'll chase these whims in this curious night,
With humor as my guide, everything feels right.
Wrapped in good cheer, with mysteries near,
I'll sway with the shadows and have a good cheer!

Ephemeral Whispers of Tomorrow

A feather floats by, a message, perhaps,
From future squirrels staging their chaps?
The sun peeks out, playing hide-and-seek,
With giggles and whispers, it's never too bleak!

My plant just winks, do you think it can chat?
Or is it a prank? Oh, the fun of that!
Hands in the dirt, and a trowel that sings,
Ephemeral whispers like magical flings!

I stare at clouds, do they know I'm awake?
Do they judge my thoughts, or simply partake?
As dreams drift and dance, I sip on my brew,
Tomorrow's conundrum, it's waiting for you!

With smiles and laughter, I greet the unknown,
In the garden of wonders, I've happily grown.
With whispers and giggles, I dance with a cheer,
A future so bright, what's there left to fear?

The Dance of Hidden Truths

In a suit of riddles, we all prance,
Twisting, twirling in a cosmic dance.
With truth as slippery as a bar of soap,
We slide and laugh, holding on to hope.

Questions like confetti float through the air,
We chase them down without a care.
The answers hide like socks in a wash,
Only to pop up with a goofy posh.

We shout, "Is that steak or a clever ploy?"
While pondering life's scheme as a giant toy.
So bring on the jests, and let's not be curbed,
For mysteries make the best jokes unheard.

Reflections in a Mysterious Pond

Skipping stones, thoughts ripple wide,
Mirror images smile, but they also hide.
The frogs croak wisdom, but I can't decode,
While the dragonflies dart like they own the road.

What's lurking below? A secretive fish?
A genie, perhaps, granting my wish?
To understand the depth of this pond so clear,
Or just catch dinner? It's all quite unclear!

A curious owl hoots, piquing my ear,
With questions so weird, it's hard not to cheer.
The water reflects stories, both near and far,
In this pond of giggles, we're all a bizarre.

Beneath the Mask of Time

Time wears a mask, not a hat or a crown,
It grins and it frowns, turning smiles upside down.
As I scribble notes on the back of my hand,
The clock giggles, "Oh, isn't this grand?"

Hours like rabbits hop off in a race,
While I'm stuck here, lost in my space.
"Why so serious?" the calendar sneers,
When I can't recall what I did for years.

Tick-tock is the tune; it's a wacky refrain,
With minutes that tease like a carnival train.
A rollercoaster ride, with me losing track,
But laughter's the ticket, so I'll go back!

Unraveled by the Moonlight

The moon winks down like a cheeky chap,
As shadows play games in this nighttime map.
With stars as our audience, we plot and we scheme,
Unraveling truths like a whimsical dream.

"Is that a ghost or just my silly hat?"
In moonlit mischief, we giggle and chat.
The darkness cuddles secrets, warm and tight,
But under the moon, they're all out of sight.

Life's jests and jabs, like a playful tune,
We dance on the paths lit by the moon.
So let's wear our quirks like badges of fun,
In this playful world, we've only begun!

The Language of Silence

In whispers soft, a secret's told,
But who speaks first? The young or old?
A nod, a wink, can say so much,
Yet I still wonder about that touch.

The squirrels chatter, the owls blink,
What are they saying? I start to think.
As crickets play their serenade,
Do they know the games we've played?

The shadows dance, the moon plays coy,
A silent partner, or is it joy?
With every grin that goes unwritten,
Do secrets slip while we're all smitten?

So talk away, you inky night,
Just keep your silence out of sight.
For in this world of code and cue,
The more you know, the less is true!

Chasing Shadows in the Twilight

I chased a shadow down the street,
It giggled, danced, on little feet.
I asked it where it's tried to roam,
It said, 'Not far, I'm still at home!'

A friendly chat with dusk's embrace,
Those darkened figures running a race.
They leap and bound without a care,
While I just trip on my own hair!

Who knew that I was made of doubt?
But shadows whisper, 'There's no route.'
They wink and tease with carefree glee,
As I get lost—just let me be.

So here I run, in circles tight,
Chasing phantoms into the night.
And maybe, just maybe, we all confound,
Life's better in circles round and round!

When Stars Speak in Riddles

The stars convene in the night sky,
Each one with tales of why and why.
They wink and nod with glinting eyes,
But their riddles? Quite the surprise!

One asked me if I liked my job,
Another laughed, 'You need to sob!'
With cosmic jokes that fall like rain,
Is laughter bright or is it pain?

But seriously now, what's up there?
Are they just lights or do they care?
Parsing through the happiness and fear,
I wish they'd text me—oh so near!

Yet in their twinkle, there's a game,
To riddle me, and I can't be blamed.
So here I sit beneath the stars,
Deciphering jokes from afar!

Portals to the Unknown

I found a door that led to space,
But it was just my dog's small face.
He barked at ghosts from way back when,
Who knew they were just neighborhood men?

With each new turn, I twist and stare,
Expecting wonders of truths laid bare.
Instead, it's all just dusty charms,
And lots of laughter in open arms.

I peered inside a box of dreams,
But all I found were tangled seams.
A portal made of sock and shoe,
Who knew knots could make me feel anew?

So let's explore the hidden lanes,
Skip along through puddles and rain.
In every corner, a jesting scene,
The unknown's fun, or so it seems!

The Curious Echo of Dreams

In a world where socks go rogue,
And turtles drive the cars,
We ponder fish in top hats,
While dancing under stars.

The banana peels provide the laughs,
As we trip through time and space,
With jellybeans as our compass,
Navigating this wild race.

Between the giggles and the sighs,
We search for answers near and far,
As marshmallows float like clouds,
And donuts lead to bizarre.

So let's embrace the silly quest,
To find out what we'll never know,
For wisdom hides in cake and jest,
While life puts on a show.

A Journey Through the Unsaid

They say there's magic in silence,
Where phrases dance on air,
With the coyness of a kitten,
Darting here and there.

Clouds whisper secrets to the trees,
While worms take notes below,
As ants plot their social schemes,
In a line, they march and go.

To ponder what's not uttered,
Is to write our own big play,
With puns that tickle fancy,
In the quirkiest ballet.

So let's scribble all the mysteries,
On napkins soaked in tea,
And share our thoughts with turtles,
Chasing dreams, wild and free.

Hidden Gardens of the Heart

Within the heart, a garden grows,
With flowers made of quirks,
Where giggles bloom like daisies,
And puns dance in the works.

A scarecrow dreams of travel,
While cacti wear a grin,
And ladybugs hold meetings,
In a shed where jokes begin.

The roses keep their secrets close,
While violets share their tunes,
As butterflies craft postcards,
To send to far-off moons.

So wander through these petals bright,
With laughter as your guide,
For in this patch of whimsy,
Our hearts can softly glide.

In Search of the Unfathomable

With goggles on and snorkels too,
We dive in thoughts so deep,
Searching for the mysteries,
That tickle us in sleep.

Each riddle wrapped in giggles,
Like puppies in a pile,
We chase after the answers,
With a gleeful, silly smile.

A goldfish wears a monocle,
While pondering the stars,
And cupcakes hold discussions,
On what's behind the bars.

So let's explore the baffling,
With laughter as our boast,
For in the land of whims and winks,
We'll always find the most.

The Breath of Infinity

In the midst of giggles, we search high and low,
Where answers are hiding, putting on a show.
With a wink and a nod, mysteries appear,
Like sock thieves at night, oh dear, oh dear!

We ponder and ponder, with a curious cheer,
Why did the chicken cross? To launch her career!
Jokes like these linger, like clouds in the sky,
Yet we laugh and we chortle, as time slips by.

In the grand cosmic joke, we're all part of the play,
With punchlines and props tucked just out of way.
So let's frolic and fumble through questions we share,
Grinning wide at the puzzle, unaware of the snare!

For in every tickle of laughter's embrace,
Lies a jest on existence, a whimsical chase.
So grab a balloon, let the silliness flow,
And dance through the chaos, let merriment grow!

Unwritten Fables

Once upon a time, in a land full of quirks,
Lived a cow playing cards, she had all of the perks.
What's the moral of this? No one really knows,
But laughter erupts, as absurdity grows.

We scribble our stories in whimsical tones,
With talking giraffes and some acid-washed phones.
Chasing peach-flavored chimeras on the run,
Leaving trails of giggles, oh what silly fun!

A riddle, a puzzle, all set in the dark,
With a frog on a skateboard, singing loud: "Let's park!"
In tales left untold, we find hidden zest,
As the punchlines unfold, we laugh with the best.

So let's spin some yarns, let the fables confide,
In the absurdity vast, let's take a joyride.
With wit as our guide, we'll leap and we'll sway,
Finding humor in stories that sparkle and play!

Illumination Beyond Sight

In shadows we wander, with lanterns so bright,
Chasing after shadows, in the dead of night.
With a giggle and gig, we twiddle our thumbs,
Sparking dreams like fireflies; oh, how fun it hums!

A light bulb goes off, but it's lit by a cat,
Wearing tiny shades, where's the sense in that?
Yet through fizzled-out fears and chuckles that soar,
We uncover the goofy, the wise, and the lore.

When the universe winks, it's a cosmic delight,
With jokes flung like stars, they twinkle so bright.
In the vastness we fumble, and missteps are round,
Yet we wear our mischief like crowns, firmly bound!

So dance, you bright souls, like shadows in flight,
Illuminated chaos, in the moonlight's might.
For in every chuckle, and twist on the grind,
Is a truth wrapped in joy that's kindly defined!

Crossroads of the Unexplained

At the intersection of never and maybe,
Stands a llama in sunglasses, looking quite wavy.
He says with a wink, "What's next on the scheme?"
As we puzzle together, lost in the dream.

Should we choose the option that leads to more fun?
Or follow the path where the clock's always run?
With confusion and laughter, we flounder and dive,
Dancing to questions that tickle and thrive.

On one side a sign says, "Go chase the unknown,"
While whispers from goose keep us twirled like a cone.
In this quirky junction, we flip a loose coin,
Hoping fortune will land on the silliness we join.

So here at this crossroad, let's chuckle and play,
As we strut through the mystery, come what may.
With joy as our compass, and laughter our guide,
We'll dance through the madness, hearts open wide!

Cadence of Continuous Wonder

In the dance of each day, we twirl and spin,
Chasing answers we lose, where do we begin?
With socks that don't match and a cat on the run,
We ponder the riddles, oh, just for fun!

Is it cheese that brings joy or just not enough sleep?
A world full of questions, a bag full of peep!
With every misstep, we chuckle and fall,
Finding wisdom in mishaps, we laugh through it all.

Towards the Undefined Horizon

We set sail at dawn on a boat made of dreams,
While the seagulls debate, or so it seems.
With a compass that's broken and snacks piled high,
The journey is wild, and so is the pie!

The stars wink above, like they know what's best,
Every twist a new laugh, every turn a jest.
We chase the horizon, what's beyond? Who knows?
But we toast with our juice, as adventure flows!

Threads that Bind Us in Inquiry.

In the tapestry woven with laughter and quirks,
We ask all the right questions, but forget how it works.
With threads of confusion and yarns of delight,
We stitch up our answers by the glow of the night.

Knitting together our thoughts and our dreams,
We unravel the jokes, while ignoring the seams.
With puzzles and giggles, we ponder the fate,
As we dance to the rhythm of 'Is it too late?'

Echoes in the Labyrinth

In the maze of existence, we wander around,
With echoing giggles and odd insights found.
Each corner we turn brings a chuckle and sigh,
As shadows debate if we're low or high.

With a map that was drawn by a very lost friend,
We follow the whispers, so bright—yet they bend.
Is there an exit or just a fun trap?
Whatever the answer, it's time for a nap!

The Scent of Forgotten Dreams

In the attic, dust collects,
Old sweaters smell like lost regrets.
A whiff of cheese, a hint of shoe,
What do our dreams really brew?

A fortune cookie said today,
'Chase your dreams, don't drift away.'
But what if dreams have all been fed,
By pizza nights and Netflix instead?

Maybe wisdom's in the snack,
But wisdom's often out to crack.
Is meaning found in moldy bread,
Or in the crumbs of thoughts we tread?

A dance of socks, a twirl of fate,
The laundry spins, don't hesitate.
In mismatched pairs, the answers hide,
Beneath the chaos, laughter resides.

Entranced by the Unknown

A shadow lurks beneath my bed,
A sock or two, perhaps instead.
I ponder life's great secret quest,
Is it just bugs that make me stress?

The universe, a cosmic joke,
With stars and space, and things that poke.
Why's the cat so wise yet vain,
While we all drift on this absurd train?

The glittering stars, they call my name,
But all I find is a child's game.
With board games stacked and dice askew,
Is winning just a losing view?

In every riddle, just more jest,
Do we unravel, or just guess?
Amidst the blindfolds and old hats,
Is meaning squished between the mats?

Whispers from Forgotten Paths

Down old alleyways I roam,
Among the weeds and a lost comb.
Each turn I take brings wild surprise,
Perhaps the truth wears a disguise?

A squirrel chats about the sun,
"Heard the news? It's all for fun!
Just nibble on the acorn's twist,
And life's a tale you can't resist!"

Through puddles deep, the questions leap,
In rainbow socks, my thoughts I keep.
I slip and slide on fate's slick floor,
"Is truth a knock or just a door?"

The whispers tease, the winds consent,
To dance beneath my discontent.
With every step, another clue,
Where paths may lead, I haven't a view.

Twists of Time and Space

The clock ticks, tick-tock, in fright,
I've misplaced time, oh what a sight!
Last week was Friday, but today's a blur,
Did I just lose it, or was it a spur?

Thoughts spiral like pasta on my plate,
"Al dente or soft? Oh, which is fate?"
I mix and stir the whims of yesterday,
Is time just pasta slipping away?

The toaster pops like fate on track,
Burns a hint of truth, but I can't snack.
I search for meaning in a slice of bread,
But all I find is the butter spread.

With every twist, the soup simmers slow,
Do we learn, or just put on a show?
In this crazy dance with time and space,
Do we embrace the giggles and misplaced grace?

The Compass of the Heart

A compass spins without a care,
Points in circles like a bear.
They say it shows the way to roam,
But I keep losing track of home.

I ask my heart to guide me right,
It chuckles softly, then takes flight.
With each beat, it plays a game,
That silly thing, it feels so lame.

Directions blur, I grin and pout,
The more I search, the more I doubt.
It leads me to the nearest pie,
Now that's a treat, oh me, oh my!

So off I go, with glee and cheer,
Through silly paths, I've no real fear.
With laughter loud, the truth will show,
We're lost, but man, it's quite a show!

Mysteries Wrapped in Time

Time's a riddle dressed in clothes,
With pockets full of old, wise prose.
I wander through its hazy space,
Where seconds trip and blunders race.

Moments glance with playful tease,
Like slippery fish, they dart with ease.
I question clocks, they laugh and tick,
Ah, what a prank! A clever trick!

In shadows danced the hours lost,
Where puzzles bloom and fears are tossed.
Maybe I'll just sit and sip,
A cup of tea, give time a trip.

So here I sit, with thoughts abound,
In riddles deep, I spin around.
If time's a mystery, I could say,
I'll stroll through life, come what may!

The Orbit of Thought

Thoughts orbit 'round like planets bright,
They buzz and swirl, a comical sight.
One minute bliss, the next a dread,
My brain's a circus, an endless spread.

With logic masks and fantasy hats,
Ideas collide, like furry cats.
I chase them down for answers raw,
But find instead a cosmic flaw.

In galaxies where worries bloom,
I laugh aloud, dispelling gloom.
The orbs of doubt spin and twirl,
With every spin, I shake and swirl.

So here I float, in thoughts afloat,
A wobbly ship, a jolly boat.
In swirling doubts, I find my glee,
For all this chaos sets me free!

Captive to Curiosity

Curiosity's a tiny sprite,
It flits around from day to night.
With questions sharp, it pokes and prods,
My mind a maze, where thought applauds.

I ask the stars where secrets hide,
They spark and wink, they've not replied.
Each "why" and "how" just leads to more,
A treasure map to distant shore.

Adventure calls on every clue,
Will fairies giggle? Who knew?
I tap my chin and ponder deep,
While goblins sneak, and shadows creep.

With humor, I chase each strange thought,
What willy-nilly lessons are taught?
So let me play, no need to flee,
For in my heart, the world's a spree!

www.ingramcontent.com/pod-product-compliance
Lightning Source LLC
Chambersburg PA
CBHW071834160426
43209CB00003B/293

*9 7 8 1 8 0 5 6 6 1 6 2 7 *